S0-BDM-408

Connie Christmas
5 Townsend Rd.
Lynnfield, Ma.

334-4395

T A for Families

T A
for
Families

**Using Transactional Analysis
for a Happier Family Life**

Adelaide Bry

Illustrations by Karen M. Schwoerer

PERENNIAL LIBRARY
Harper & Row, Publishers
New York, Hagerstown, San Francisco, London

T A FOR FAMILIES. Text copyright © 1976 by Adelaide Bry. Illustration copyright © 1976 by Karen M. Schwoerer

All rights reserved. Printed in the United States of America. No part of this book may be used or reproduced in any manner without written permission except in the case of brief quotations embodied in critical articles and reviews. For information address Harper & Row, Publishers, Inc., 10 East 53d Street, New York, N.Y. 10022. Published simultaneously in Canada by Fitzhenry & Whiteside Limited, Toronto.

Designed by Eve Callahan

First PERENNIAL LIBRARY edition published 1976

LIBRARY OF CONGRESS CATALOG CARD NUMBER: 75–29650

STANDARD BOOK NUMBER: 06–080365–7

76 77 78 79 80 10 9 8 7 6 5 4 3 2

My very special thanks to special T A people

Mary and Bob Goulding
Jack Dusay for his Egogram
Steven Karpman for the Karpman triangle
Herb Hamsher

Introduction

This book is for you,
if you need some help in making your family
relationships work better;
whether you are
married or unmarried
a mother or a father
a son or a son-in-law
a daughter or a daughter-in-law
a mother-in-law or a father-in-law
or a grandparent.

Share this book with that important person in your
life (that you just might be having problems with)
and you'll discover that you and that "other person"
can solve your difficulties and have more joy, too!

_____

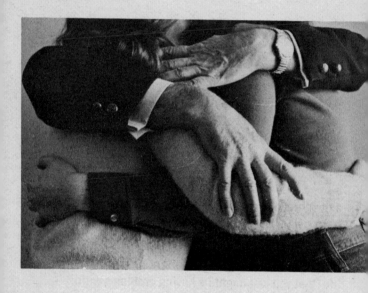

6

Sometimes a relationship
sounds like this

"I absolutely adore you."
"I think you're the greatest!"

(This is whether the relationship is between you and
your mother, you and your husband or wife,
you and your child,
you and your sister or brother,
you and your grandchild.)

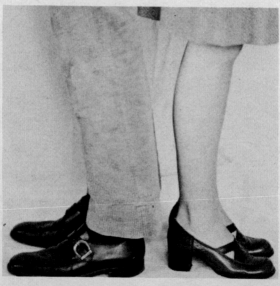

And sometimes other kinds of feelings
creep in.

"You don't understand me. You understand my younger
sister better than me."
"It's no fun being with *you*."
"I don't feel happy in this family."
"Nobody loves me anymore."

THIS CERTIFICATE

ENTITLES YOU TO

ABSOLUTE AND PERFECT

LOVE .

HEY, THAT'S NOT REAL.

Whoever said that family life should be
sweet music and soft lights and complete joy
every single day is just being plain silly,
but the degree and kinds of problems you have
all depend upon what you learned when you were
a little boy or a little girl.

Nobody *gets* perfect love. But your family can
probably be happier than they are, now.
But each person in the family has to work at it.

On this very page you can decide to make
a relationship work
or
you can sit and wait
for
Santa Claus.*

* People who have their heads up in the clouds
waiting for something to happen
sit and sit
wait and wait
like little kids on Christmas Eve.

Jane:
"i'd like to go to the seashore."

TOM:

Instead of waiting for Santa Claus,
you and that other person can
learn to talk the same language,
the T A language.

T A ?
T A is a good way to help you understand
why and how
you react to certain people in certain ways.

(Ever feel that you're not understood, that
other people in your family don't get your message?)

A TRANSACTION

is COMMUNICATING

WITH SOMEONE ELSE.

In the T A language, every single time
you talk
and the other person answers
you are having a transaction.

You give words and feelings.
You get words and feelings.

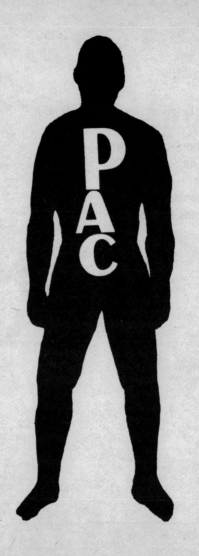

The ABCs of the T A language
are called
P
A
C

P stands for Parent
A stands for Adult
C stands for Child

ARE YOU MORE OFTEN
NURTURING
OR
CRITICAL ?

Say, what's a Parent? (In this new T A language.)

A Parent is everything you were *taught* by
   your mother and father or whoever brought you up.
   And all that P you learned is inside of you, right
   this minute!

Your P has two parts (just divide the P circle in half).
   Nurturing Parent means you care for yourself and
      other people
      (it does not mean you are a mommy or daddy).
   Critical Parent means you are critical, you are bossy
      (and this, too, has nothing to do with actually
      being a mommy or daddy).

21

ARE YOU MORE OfTEN
fREE AND **hAppy**
OR
SAd AND **ANGRy ?**

22

Now, what's a Child? (In this new T A language.)

Your Child is what you *feel* inside.
Your C has two parts (just divide the C circle in half).

Free Child means you are fun-loving, curious, creative.
   (It does not mean you are young in years
   like 3 or 4.)
Adaptive Child means you are sad, angry, depressed.
   (Your Adaptive Child is operating at any
   age, 6 or 60.)

Right in the middle is the big letter that
will make your relationships work better.

The Big
    A (for Adult)
is the window of your reality.

The Big
    A
looks at what is going on now and makes *real-life
decisions.*

(When two people are having trouble with each other
they need to focus on their A.)

The Big
    A
needs to be in good working condition all the time.

The Big
    A
is logical, down-to-earth, is not emotional.

Sometimes heavy, critical Ps overshadow the As
and the Cs.
The best communication
takes into account
    your feelings in your C,
    your thoughts in your A,
    and what you learned in your P.
All your PACs are important.

right now
figure out your

P
A
C

about the
most important relationship
in your life

Sometimes, when a girl/boy decide to get married,
the PAC talk (inside of one person or the other)
might go something like this:

P: Mommy and Daddy will like the person I've picked.
    Same religion, hard worker; that's what they
    wanted for me.

A: I'm ready to make a lifetime commitment. I'll
    weather the problems.

C: I love ——. I feel so wonderful when we're
    together.

PUT YOUR ANSWERS HERE

What do you do today that is   P
"just the way Mom and Dad did it" a long
time ago?

What decision did you make today that was   A
logical and down-to-earth?

What did you do today that was fun? Or angry?   C

If you love your grandmother
right this very minute
and your grandmother
loves you
both of you are in your
        free, happy C to C

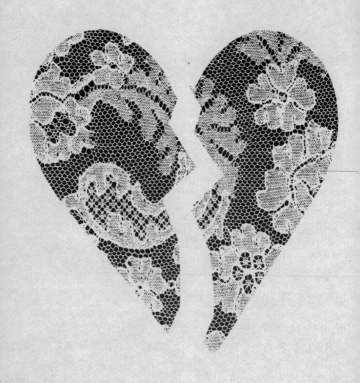

Sometimes CPs come out strong (from anyone in the family: Mother, Father, Aunt Susie, Grandmother).

Be quiet.

You should get home on time.

You ought to clean better.

Do your homework right now.

Love seems to vanish and somebody's heart gets broken when there are too many CPs.

If you're the person in a family who gets "put down"
a lot your feelings get stormy.
All kinds of things are going on inside your head.

Your P says,

Stick it out. That's the right way.

Your A says,

Let's work at it together.

Your C says,

I feel terrible. I'd like to run away.

The big relationship wrecker is when you don't
talk
A to A about all kinds of things
like:

money
children
where to live
holidays
friends
in-laws.

Keep your A in good working order.

Funny, when your A to A doesn't work,
then all that blissful happy fun you were
        having in your C to C just seems to vanish.
The trouble is everyday life isn't like a fairy tale.

There is no prince with a glass slipper,
and no perfect mommy or perfect daddy.
(Not *even* perfect children.)

When you are with someone all the time
you have all kinds of
transactions.

Some are loving.
    You're great.
    I love you too.

Some are put-downs.
    You're mean.
    I hate you.

Some don't work at all.
    Where is my tie?
    Don't ask me.
    (That question never even got answered.)

Feelings and words you didn't know were there spill out
sometimes, like something boiling over.

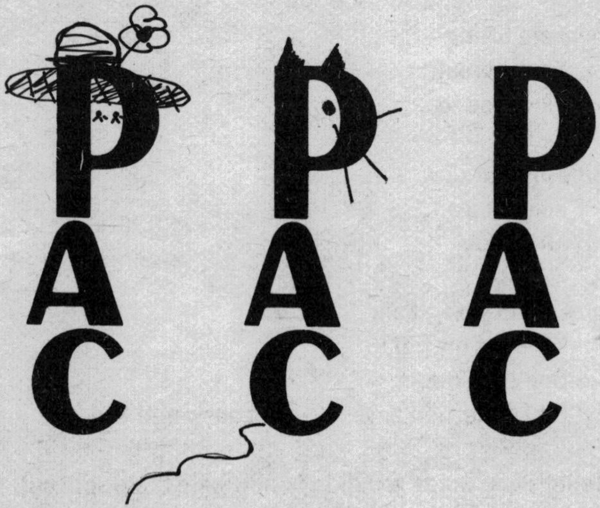
PAC
PAC
PAC

In your family, think for just a minute
of all the
P
A
C
going on inside each person all the time.

When you shake your fist at your sister, and
she sticks out her tongue at you, that's a transaction.

When you point your finger at your daughter and say,
    "Go to your room," and she starts to cry, that's
    a transaction.

When you say to your husband,
    "I love you," and your husband answers with a hug,
    that's a transaction.

The Rule: When you say or do something to another
    person or an animal, and you get a response (with
    or without words) you are having a transaction.

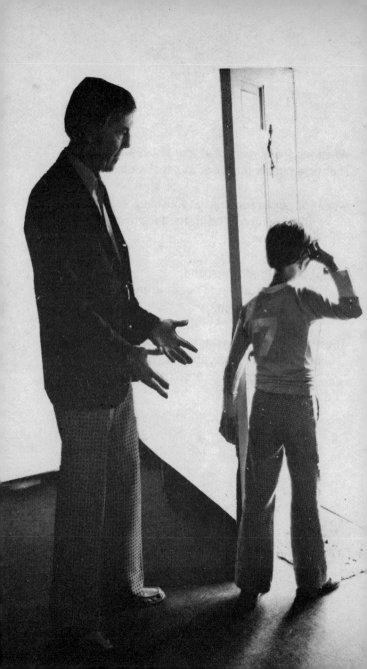

When Dad says to Tim,
"You have to stay home and do your homework,"
but Tim answers by
walking out the door, that becomes a
crossed transaction. It doesn't work.

(Dad is the Critical Parent, talking down to Tim's C.
But Tim refused to answer, "Yes, Dad, I'll do what you
want," and walked out instead.)

When Sally (age 5) and John (age 8) are playing mommy and daddy, and pretending they're going off on a visit to take care of their married daughter who just had a baby, they're both being Nurturing Parents in this transaction.

(It doesn't matter how old you are. It's what you do and feel that decides whether you're in your P, your A, or your C.)

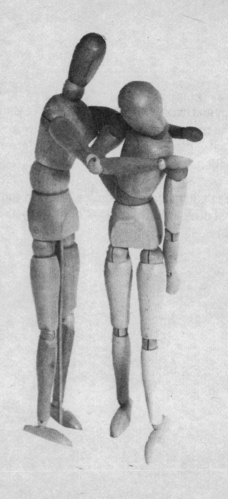

Sometimes, one grownup needs to feel he or she is being taken care of by another grownup.

    She: Help me. I really need you to help me.
    He: I will.

He's Nurturing Parent.
She's Child.

Now, is that good or bad, right or wrong?
It's perfectly OK, the transaction is working.
It's a *complementary* transaction.

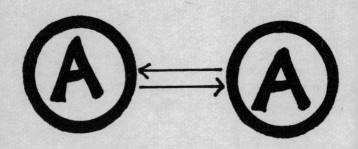

A simple Adult to Adult transaction goes like this:

Wife: Jim, please mow the lawn.

Husband: OK.

(That's a transaction that works. The lines are straight.)

she   he

Here's one that *doesn't* work.

Wife: Jim, please mow the lawn.
Husband: Why do you always ask me? I don't want to.
(You remind me of my mother, always telling me what to do.)

(This is a crossed transaction.)

Does this ever happen at your house?

Sam said to Mother: Sally tore up my picture. Punish her.

Mother said to Sam: Be *nice* to Sally. She's just a baby.

(Sam feels both sad and angry. He didn't get a real answer from Mother).

Mother could have answered in many ways:

I'll tell Sally never to do that again.

Let's see how we can keep your pictures out of her reach.

Sure, you want her punished, you're angry with her.

Tell her you're angry and I will, too.

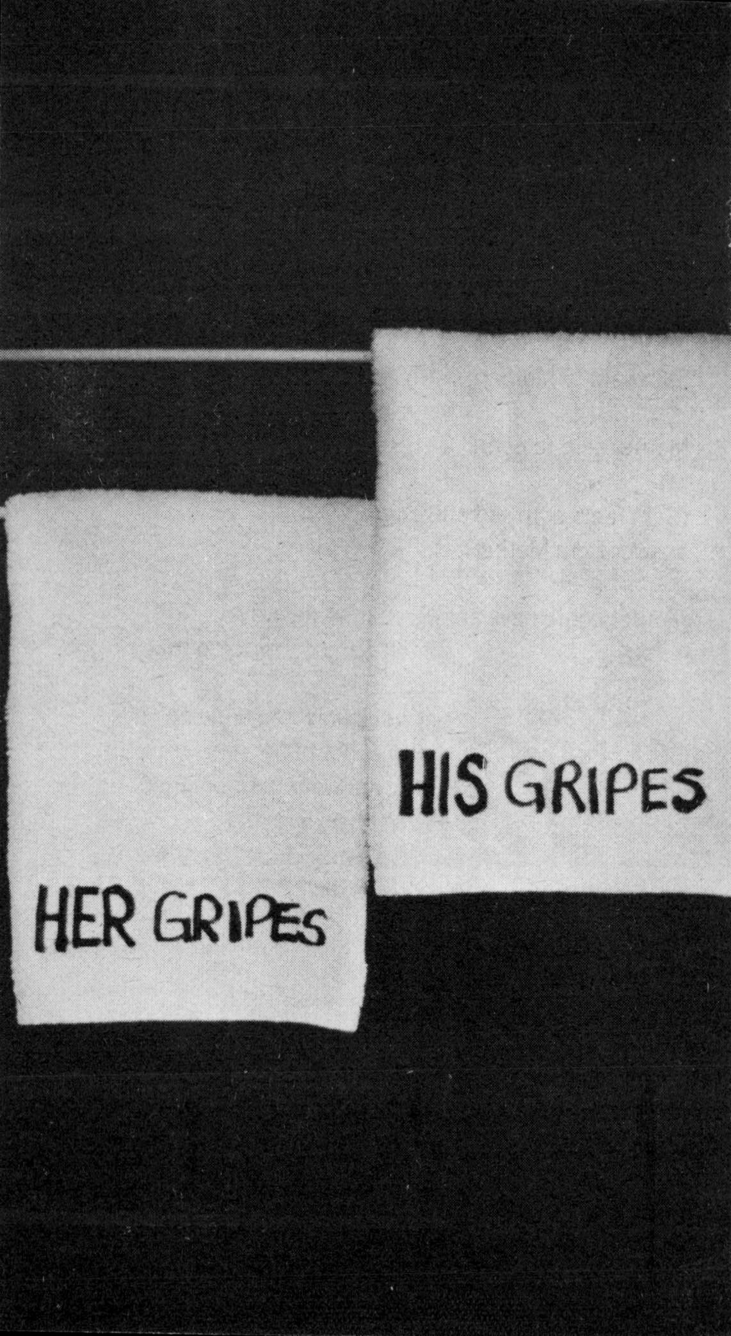
HIS GRIPES
HER GRIPES

Sit down right now (whatever your age) and put all
your As out on the table.
When you do that you
make a list of
    —   his/her gripes
        your gripes
and then ask in your A
"What can we do to make it better?"

Whatever in the world do you do when two ACs
are feeling simply awful?
My AC sometimes gets depressed and cries.
My AC is sometimes angry.

Move up one into your A.
There you start looking at your Ps and Cs.

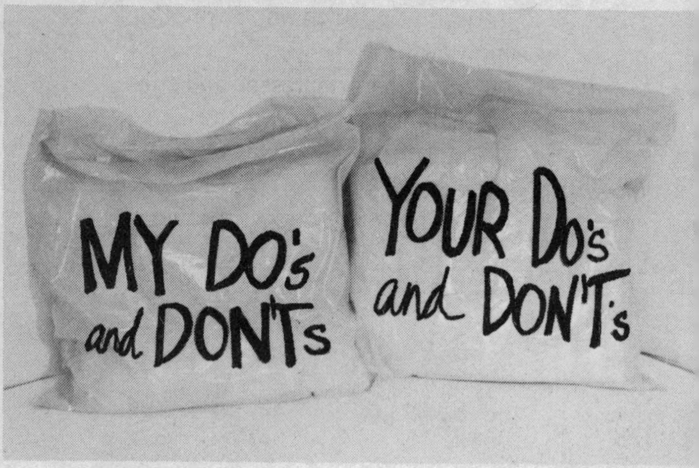
MY DO's and DONTs
YOUR Do's and DON'T's

At the very beginning of every relationship,
each person comes with an invisible but heavy
sack just stuffed with
do's
and
don'ts from *their* parents:
special ways of doing things (Sunday dinner at noon or
night), and all the feelings you had when you were very
little.
(These are the Ps.)

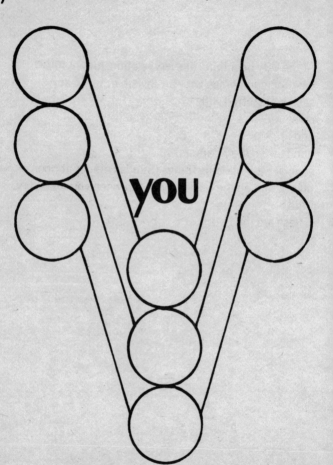

What you learned from your mother and your father
is your life-script.

What did you learn when you were little about
what was
>   good or bad to feel about sex?
>   good or bad about eating chocolate or pizza?
>   good or bad to be a fireman or a lawyer when you
>   grew up?

You are a combination of their PACs,
which make up your PAC.

Think right now what you learned and what
he/she learned:

Keep the house neat. (He learned.)
Relax, let it be messed up. Who cares?
(She learned.)

Too much meat isn't good for you. (She learned.)
A dinner without meat isn't a real dinner.
(He learned.)

That's how two people get into trouble . . .
each person's learning, when they were little, is
just a little different, and each person feels he/she
has the RIGHT way.

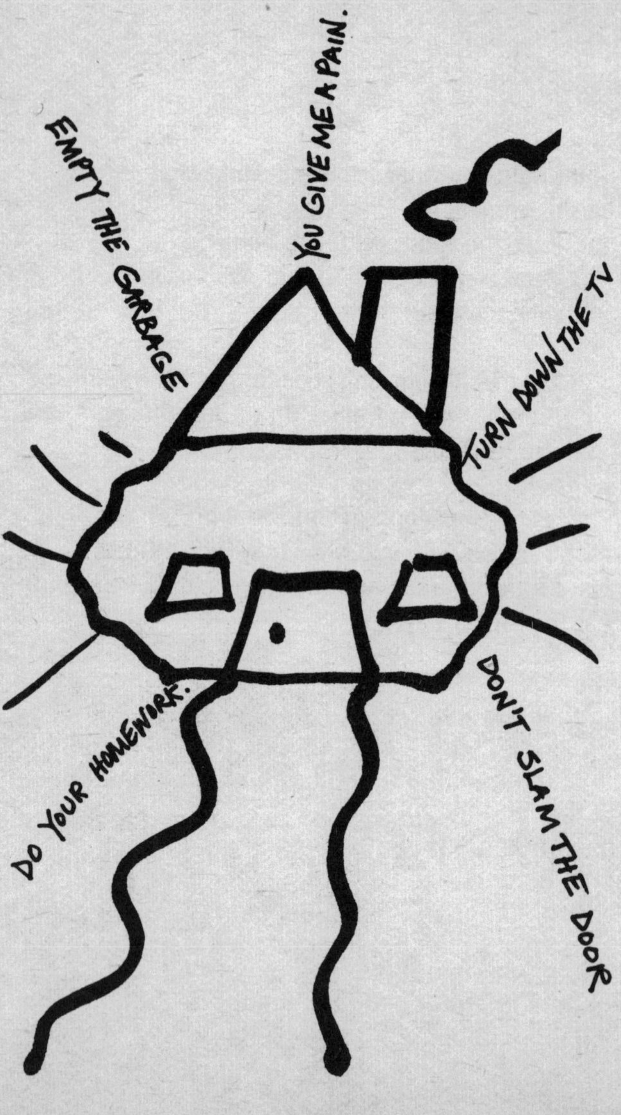
EMPTY THE GARBAGE
YOU GIVE ME A PAIN.
TURN DOWN THE TV
DON'T SLAM THE DOOR
DO YOUR HOMEWORK.

How in the world can couples and families
live together in one house and each other's
particular
"RIGHT WAY"
and ever ever have it work?

RECEIPE FAMILY MIX		SERVES
INGREDIENTS	ONE MOTHER	
	ONE FATHER	
	ONE BOY, 5	
	ONE GIRL, 7	
	ONE GRANDMOTHER, 63	

DIRECTIONS

PUT IN BLENDER, ADD TA, AND MIX WELL.

Favorite recipe of TA

WHEW!

(Nobody said it was a cinch,
but . . . it can be better than it is.)

What's your family mix?
    good
    bad   (Check one.)
    awful

injunctions:
keep   discard

What did your mother and father tell you long ago,
or only yesterday? Did they tell you:

    Jim, you're an OK kid.

    Marlene, you're not very smart.

    Jane, marry young, have lots of kids.

    Bill, if you don't make a lot of money, life is no
    good.

Make a list of the "right ways" you
learned when you were little.

The T A word for these "right ways" is "injunction."

Then make two piles, one: the injunctions you want to
keep and two: the injunctions you want to throw away.

P.S. Don't hang on to old "right ways" that are silly
    right now.

what old injunction is hurting your relationship right this minute?

In some families, children and grownups are afraid to be close and warm and loving, just because the grownups learned that *that* was scary when *they* were little.

Change it now, today.
Tell someone in your family when you feel good about him/her.
Hug someone in your family when you feel good about him/her.

What *old* injunction is hurting your relationship right this minute?

Up until this minute, which one applied to you?
    I can give lots of love and gets lots of love.
    I can give practically no love and I don't get much either.

Isn't it strange, in some families there is
    one grandmother everyone adores and
    one grandmother who is very hard to get along with.
      (Her own daughter will be the first to admit it.)

(Some grandmothers stay in their A, have fun with the
grandchildren in their happy Child, are nurturing Ps.
They're helpful and kind.

But . . . other grandmothers are mean and bossy;
they're in the CP *all* the time.

That's when a daughter-in-law says, "I can't bear to
pick up the telephone. It's always Jim's mother, telling
me what to do.")

When you pay attention to someone,
you're *stroking*. (In T A.)

Ever think that even when you're angry at someone,
you're still paying attention to him—that's stroking, too!

The very worst thing that can happen is not to be
noticed at all. It's as though you were invisible.

One way of getting attention is to
discount someone.
Did someone ever talk to you as though
you were worth exactly one cent?

(That's negative stroking in T A.)

MOTHER:
FATHER:
CHILDREN:

1.
2.
3.
4.

P	N	C
O	E	O
S	G	N
I	A	D
T	T	I
I	I	T
V	V	I
E	E	O
		N
		A
		L

WHO WINS?

Get the whole family to start counting strokes for one day.

Make a list:

    Positive strokes—I like you.

    Negative strokes—I don't like you.

    Conditional strokes—I like you when you do
                            something
                            I want you to do.

After dinner, sit down and have a stroke-counting session.

P
A
C

WHAT

NOT ok feelings

ARE GETTING INTO

YOUR RELATIONShip

?

The kind of loving you give and the kind of loving you get all depends upon how you feel about you.

There are only four basic ways. Which is your way?
    I'm OK, you're OK:
        Healthy; your relationship will get closer.
    I'm OK, you're not OK:
        You blame the other person: divorce, separate.
    I'm not OK, you're OK:
        You feel helpless; you may run away from your relationship.
    I'm not OK, you're not OK:
        You feel you can't win no matter what you do.

Do you ever feel (just to yourself, of course):
    If he/she cared more about me, then I'd be OK.
    If I were beautiful, rich, handsome, bright,
        amusing, then I'd be OK.
It doesn't work that way. OK-ness is all inside of you.

You are the boss of you (whether you are 5 or 35)
and you can begin now to use your Big A to
decide you're OK. Cut out those *ifs* right now.

When families are having trouble,
it's often because they don't
listen to each other.

They don't plug in their
Adult.
Each person has so much emotion inside
he/she doesn't
listen to what's going on outside.

WHAT bROUGHT yOU THE MOST REWARds WHEN yOU WERE little?

A little kid learns early to do what works—
like crying if that brings love, stroking.

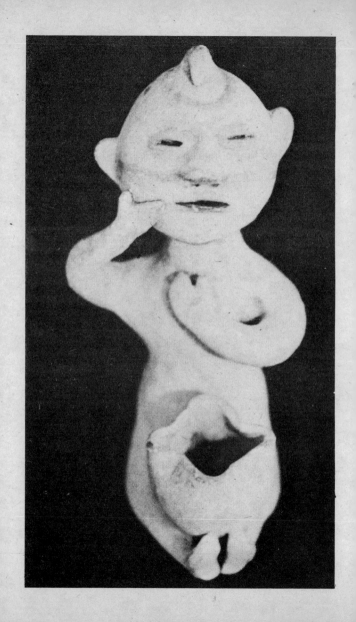

If today you're 18, 28, or even 68, you're carrying around all those ways you learned to feel when you were little.

> And that can include keeping quiet, being depressed, hating everyone, loving, laughing, never speaking up.

What in heaven's name is a
NORMAL
family?

(Everyone always asks that question.)

WE'RE ALL HUMAN
AND
WE ALL MAKE
MISTAKES.

A normal family is:

    Each family member feeling he can manage his life.

    (If you're a child reading this book, you do what you can do for your age.)

    Having respect for each person in the family, young and old.

    Feeling you can talk to the other members of your family and they will listen.

    Feeling you can listen to the other members of your family and they can talk.

    Feeling you give and get some love.

P.S. None of this works perfectly all the time.

But sometimes we get hurt when we are little.
It feels like someone put a lid on our heads.
And then we put a lid on our children's heads.
And then they go on putting a lid on their children's
heads.
On and on . . .

Unless a family joins together to look at what they
are doing to themselves and to each other,
they simply go on in the same old way.

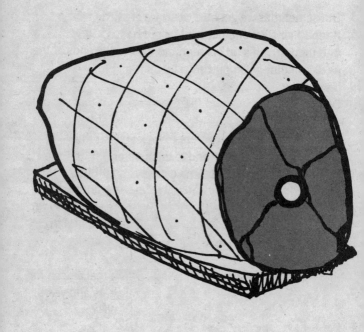

This is a true story: A young bride
decided to bake a ham for her husband.
Before putting it into the pan, she cut off the ends of the
ham.
Her husband asked why.
"Because," she replied, "my mother does it that way."
Her husband asked his mother-in-law why she
cut off the ends of the ham.
And she replied, "Because *my* mother does it that way."
So he asked the grandmother why *she* cut off the
ends of the ham before baking it, and the grandmother
replied, "When I was first married we were very poor, we
only had one pan and it was a small one, and I had to cut
the ends off so the ham would fit into the pan."

The moral: Once upon a time there was a real reason for
doing what she did, but for years and years,
no one ever bothered to ask WHY.

WHY ??

Start now to ask some WHYS.

> Why does my sister always slam the door on me?
> Why does Tim run to his room when his sister picks
> on him?
> Why is little sister getting bad grades in school
> when she got good ones last year?
> Why is Dad coming home later these days?
> Why is Mother having a lot of "crying spells"?
> Why is it I'm the person who always seems to "get
> it"?
> Why does my daughter-in-law refuse to come to
> dinner?
> Why doesn't anyone in this family enjoy each other?

What's real right now?

You may not want to look at some of the
answers you hear
while you are "tracking down"
what's going on in your family.

Your goal: Each family member feels he's OK,
            has his own rights, shares with
            the others, too.

It's not just what you *say* that counts.
Pretend you have an invisible rope going
from you to each person in the family, and they
each in turn have one going to you and everyone else.

Sometimes actions do speak louder than words.
Sometimes a look really does hurt.

In a family, the others know what you're feeling; after
all, you're together practically every day for years and
years.

do WHAT YOU WANT i DON'T CARE.

Transactions go on and on in:
    body language,
    the words you use,
    your tone of voice.

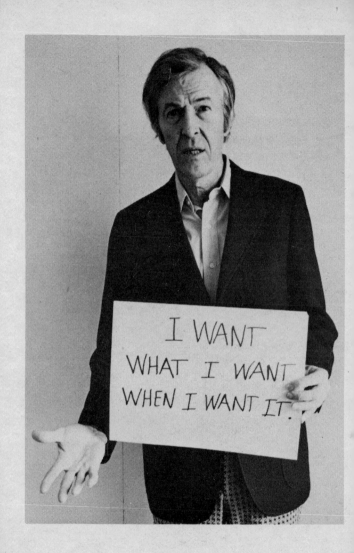

A good trackdown on a quiet Sunday is to ask
each member of the family or your partner
(if there are just two of you) how each one feels
about . . . almost anything.

Surprise: Most of us see it *our* way.

TRACK dOWN YOUR ANGER iN YOUR A

Jeannie used to fight with her mother all the time.
She tracked down that when she slammed the door,
her mother felt hurt like a little girl just six years old.
(And then no one talked for days.)
They did the trackdown in their A, calmly, as they
decided that to go on repeating

    door slamming
    mother feeling hurt

was really silly, because it was the same old thing.
It turned out that Jeannie, 15, was the Critical
Parent and mother was being the Angry Child.

Debby and Bobby were always fighting for Dad's attention.

> Debby: I'm smarter than you are.
> Bobby (in tears): You can't do anything. And, anyhow,
> Dad likes me better.

They tracked down that Dad was praising Debby a lot, and hardly ever stroked Bobby.

Dad saw that he was really making it easy for Debby and Bobby to fight a lot. Dad used his A and decided that he would give Bobby more approval.

Why? Just because Bobby was his son and was human and needed approval. That's positive stroking, no conditions.

EGOGRAM:

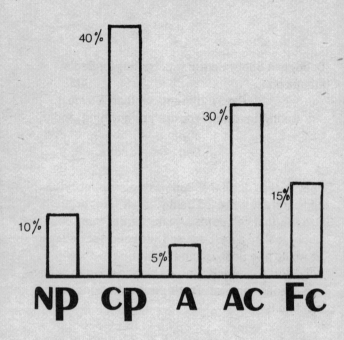

NP	CP	A	AC	FC
10%	40%	5%	30%	15%

THIS ONE IS A PICTURE OF A DAD
WHO PUTS HIS KIDS DOWN A LOT;
EVERYONE HIDES FROM Dad
WHEN HE COMES HOME.

To find out which of the PACs you spend your time in,
make a picture of yourself called an EGOGRAM.
You divide your PACs, using your logical A to do it.
(Be just as honest as you can, this is
your self-portrait.)

(Everything has to add up to 100 percent.)

On the picture page across from this page:

NP	stands for	Nurturing Parent
CP	stands for	Critical Parent
A	stands for	Adult
AC	stands for	Adaptive Child
FC	stands for	Free Child

THIS IS MY EGOGRAM:
100%

NP CP A AC HC

Here's your page to do your own EGOGRAM.
Why not have each member of the family do his/hers?

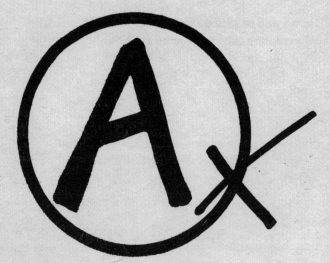

the biggest a's
aren't always
the winners.

After each person has made an EGOGRAM, compare
  notes.
Who has the biggest Critical Parent?   (CP)
Who has the biggest Free Child?   (FC)
Who acts rational and business-like
  most of the time?   (A)

If you think the person with the biggest Adult
wins, you're wrong. That doesn't make you a
WINNER.

FIRST PRIZE

if you do that,

you get first Prize.

The WINNER is a person who:
    does not play helpless,
    is not afraid to think and feel
    and be independent,
    and listens to the other person,
    and talks to the other person in
    straight down-to-earth words.
The WINNER:
    is not what someone else said
    he should be.
The WINNER:
    uses all the PACs, using the right one
    at the right time.

Winning has nothing to do with scoring points *over* someone else.

mom always Put dad down (1960)

i always Put jim down (today)

Check out your WINNER qualities.

How do the other people in the family answer you?
     You make me sick.
          or
     OK, let's work it out.

If you're a mother or father, think back to your
childhood.
     Are you doing it now the way they
     behaved to each other?
     (If Mother put Dad down, are you doing it too?)

Do you feel like a worm?

Don't squirm and feel like a worm, if you feel right now
that you don't measure up to some invisible perfection.
Keep in mind the word
MOST;
how everything works
MOST of the time.

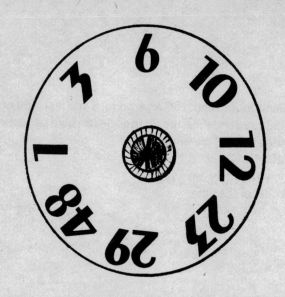

ARE YOU OFTEN
SELECTING THE
CHANNEL WITH
STATIC?

Maybe you don't realize how many options you have in your transactions? What channels are you picking? You have more than you may use.

One partner says:	The other partner has these options (and more):
	CP: About time you gave me a choice.
A Where should we go for dinner tonight?	A: I'd like to try that new Italian restaurant.
	C: I felt like going out last night. Why didn't you ask me then?

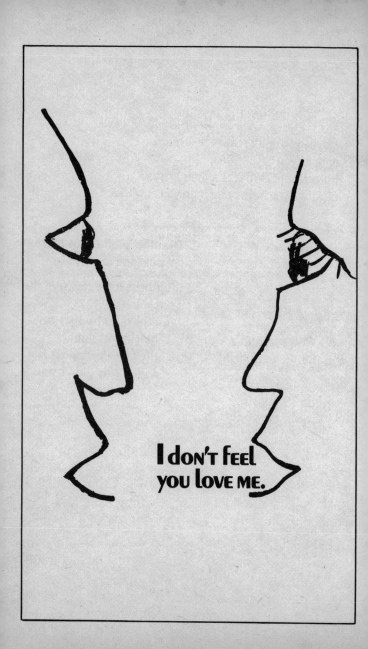

I don't feel
you love me.

One day Marge and George were having an argument.
   "I don't feel you really love me."

George had a choice of answers:

   NP (soothingly):   Of course I love you.
    A (rationally):   We keep working it out. It's OK.
    C (angrily):   I don't feel you love me.

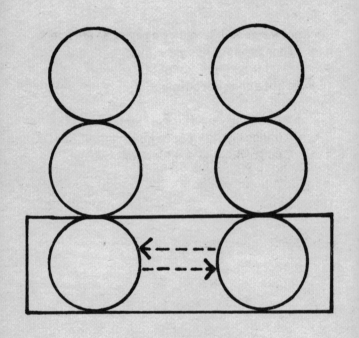

SECRET

134

The very next time you say something to someone
in the family, ask yourself:
Is that what I really mean
        or
do I have a secret message?

Out loud:
      Wife: I'm so worn out tonight.
  Husband: That's OK.

The truth:
      Wife: I don't want sex.
  Husband: I don't either.

A relationship in trouble is apt to have too much
secret communication and not enough out in the open.

He says: You always put me down.
She says: You always criticize me.

But the secret is:
He: I need you. Don't leave me.
She: I need you, too.

The secret is to unlock your secrets. Be straight.

Some guaranteed ways to
BREAK
your relationship are:

Feel cheated most of the time.
Feel that if he/she is in a bad mood, you have to be
too.
Turn down affection.
Bring up past arguments in the middle of this one.
Give in now, feel angry later.

WELL ??

Hey, what about affection?

> Do you use it? (CP)
> Do you enjoy it (NP)
> Do you withhold it? (AC)
> Do you share it? (FC)

Parents use it, enjoy it, withhold it, share it with their children.

Children do the same with their parents.

Sisters and brothers, and lovers, too, sometimes play games with their affections.

Sometimes relationships are so crammed with games
you'd think the two people were on separate teams,
each fighting for his own team to win.

The game in T A goes around in a triangle,
one person often takes two parts. Sometimes three
people play.

When you take your part, you may be scared of getting
close to your partner.

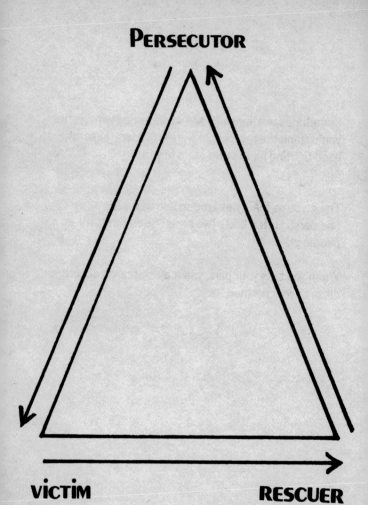

Here's a couple's game called "courtroom."

>   She: You never take me out anymore.
>   (Persecutor)
>   He: You don't like what I suggest. (Victim)
> Third player: I'm judge and jury, I'll decide what is best
>   for you both. (Rescuer)

The Rescuer may be your so-called best friend, your mother, your father-in-law.

The helper in the GAME, acting as
Rescuer, falls into the trap, too.
Nobody wins in the GAME.

Playing a game is like being wrapped in
plastic—it keeps you from real feelings.

You need warmth in your life and you go around
lonely and put down, or putting someone else down.

What fun is that? (Well, it's some fun if you don't
know any better.)

fuNNy but---
even wHen you win
you Lose.

Depending upon the way you were when you were little,
you may always choose the same role in every game.
    Like always being a Victim, or else a
    Persecutor, or else a Rescuer.

Or . . . you may like to switch around and get your kicks
out of playing *all* these roles.

The problem is,
game players
don't really win.

Game players collect what we call
"hollow triumphs."
NOT WINS. Bad feelings.
It's like cutting off your nose to spite your face.
You sure fixed your face!

It sounds silly and downright stupid, but to some people
bad feelings are better than good feelings,
because that's what they learned
once upon a time.

So, just like some people collect supermarket trading
stamps, some people collect bad-feeling trading stamps
(and the more the not-so-merrier).

Only true and honest and good
feelings work best for you. Because
you feel honestly good, not phony.

Remember the expression
"You learned it at your mother's knee."

All your important learning, all the do's and don'ts about
your feelings took place even before you went to
kindergarten.

How does that learning,
way back then,
affect you in your relationship
right this minute?

Are you putting your father's face on your husband?
Are you putting your mother's face on your wife?

Look, once again, at your partner.
See a special, unique person, not your mother or your
father or whoever brought you up.

The very best way to

> enjoy a relationship,
> keep a relationship,
> save a relationship

is to give up the search for what you think of as
TRUE LOVE.
(That's your little Adaptive Child asking your mate to
provide you with everything you got when you were little
or everything you didn't get but you wanted to get.)

If right now you see your relationship
as:

      You ought to give me more (of anything)—
        you're in your CP.

If you see it as:

      I'm a poor little unloved person—
        you're in your AC.

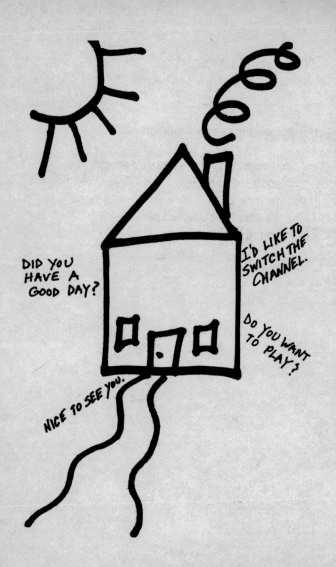

Look at what is real:
Two people, four people, seven people,
all willing to
      enjoy some fun and laughter,
      make it better,
      trust each other's feelings.

When all the members of a family put their
As in good working order and use their "free child" for
happy times, then you can all weather good
times and bad.

Maybe all this isn't as romantic as you felt true
love would be.
Working at it every day,
waking up to the mystery and beauty of life itself,
treasuring the precious moments,
reaching out a hand,
knowing you are OK just because you're alive on
      this earth and knowing that about all the
      people in your life and those you haven't even
      been introduced to yet,
knowing you are OK when you are angry and OK when
you're happy.
That's what true love is, because it's being true to you
and your family, too.

About the Author

ADELAIDE BRY is a counseling psychologist in private practice and consultant for business on communication problems. She is the author of *The Sexually Aggressive Woman* (New York: Wyden, 1975), *T A Games: Using Transactional Analysis in Your Life* (New York: Harper & Row, 1975); *A Primer of Behavioral Psychology* (New York: New American Library, 1975); *The T A Primer: Transactional Analysis in Everyday Life* (New York: Harper & Row, 1973); *Inside Psychotherapy* (New York: Basic Books, Inc., 1972), and numerous articles of psychological interest. She uses transactional analysis with groups, and the idea for *The T A Primer, T A Games,* and *T A for Families* evolved from her need to give people a simple, understandable introduction to the subject.

She is the mother of two children: Barbara, a student at Harvard Business School, and Douglas, a student at the University of Colorado Law School.

Ms. Bry lectures widely, and has appeared on Mike Douglas's, Johnny Carson's, and Lou Gordon's TV programs, and also on "Kup's Show" and AM America. She is a member of the International Transactional Analysis Association, and Association of Humanistic Psychology.

About Transactional Analysis

"I highly recommend this book for those wanting a better knowledge of people.

"The credit for this basic system of understanding yourself and others belongs to the late Dr. Eric Berne. The International Transactional Analysis Association is a world-wide organization of men and women who use these techniques."

—KENNETH EVERTS, M.D.
Past President, ITAA

For further information about transactional analysis, write to The International Transactional Analysis Association, Inc., 1772 Vallejo Street, San Francisco, California 94123.